Jamaica
MY ISLAND HOME

Adrian Mandara Ph.D.

Ages 4 – 6

Editor: K. Sean Harris
Illustrations: Courtney Robinson
Cover Design: Sanya Dockery
Book Design, Layout & Typeset: Sanya Dockery

Published by: LMH Publishing Ltd.
Suite 10-11
Sagicor Industrial Park
7 Norman Road
Kingston C.S.O, Jamaica
Tel: 876-938-0005
Fax: 876-759-8752
Email: lmhbookpublishing@cwjamaica.com
Website: www.lmhpublishing.com

Printed in China

ISBN: 978-976-8245-02-1

NATIONAL LIBRARY OF JAMAICA CATALOGUING-IN-PUBLICATION DATA

Mandara, Adrian
    Jamaica : my island home / Adrian Mandara

    p. : ill. , maps ; cm.
For children age 3-7)
ISBN 978-976-8245-02-1 (pbk)

1. Jamaica – Description and travel – Juvenile literature
2. Jamaica – Social life and customs
I . Title

917.292 - dc 22

Dedication

To all the emergent and developing readers of our lovely island.

Sweet, Sweet Jamaica

Sweet, Sweet Jamaica
Land of wood and water
Columbus and his soldiers said
it was the finest land ever seen.

The Taino Indians
The first people of Jamaica,
Friendly, honest and loving,
Loved to fish and hunt
Even planted cassava, cassava
cassava.

Then came the Great Encounter
Spaniards met the Tainos,
Tainos didn't last.

The English came,
Sugar was King
So was slavery.

Road to Emancipation,
filled with potholes of challenges
now overcome
led to the journey
to Independence.

Jamaica is Africans, Spanish,
English, Chinese, East Indians,
peoples from the Middle East
all in Sweet Jamaica.

Preface

Early in life learning to read and write begins to develop as children involve themselves in many varied activities in homes, schools and communities that involve literacy. As educators we need to accept children's emergent ways of reading and writing. Some of these are: pretending to read, drawing, scribbling, even their invented spelling. We must build on these ways so that we may help our children embrace conventional reading and writing successfully.

Jamaica My Island Home wishes to build on children's emerging and developing ways of reading and understanding by offering them an interesting, informative book about beautiful Jamaica, its people and the pride they should have in their country.

This is my

It is mine too

1

Jamaica.

KINGSTON

Jamaica is ours too.

KINGSTON

Jamaica

Lucea

Montego
Bay

Falmouth

St. Ann's
Bay

Ocho
Rios

Port
Maria

Negril

Buff
Bay

Savanna-la-Mar

Port
Antonio

Mandeville

Black
River

Spanish
Town

KINGSTON

Alligator
Pond

May
Pen

Treasure
Beach

Portmore

Morant
Bay

has many nice towns and cities.

4

Jamaica is a pretty country.

We love Jamaica.

I must keep Jamaica clean.

I must not litter.

We must not litter our houses.

We must not litter our yards.

We must not litter our schools.

We must not litter.

Our playground is a happy place.

We keep it clean.

We pick up bits of paper and other litter.

I must keep my country clean.

We must keep our country
clean.

Jamaica is an island.

t has water all around it. The water is the Caribbean Sea.

Jamaica has many mountains.

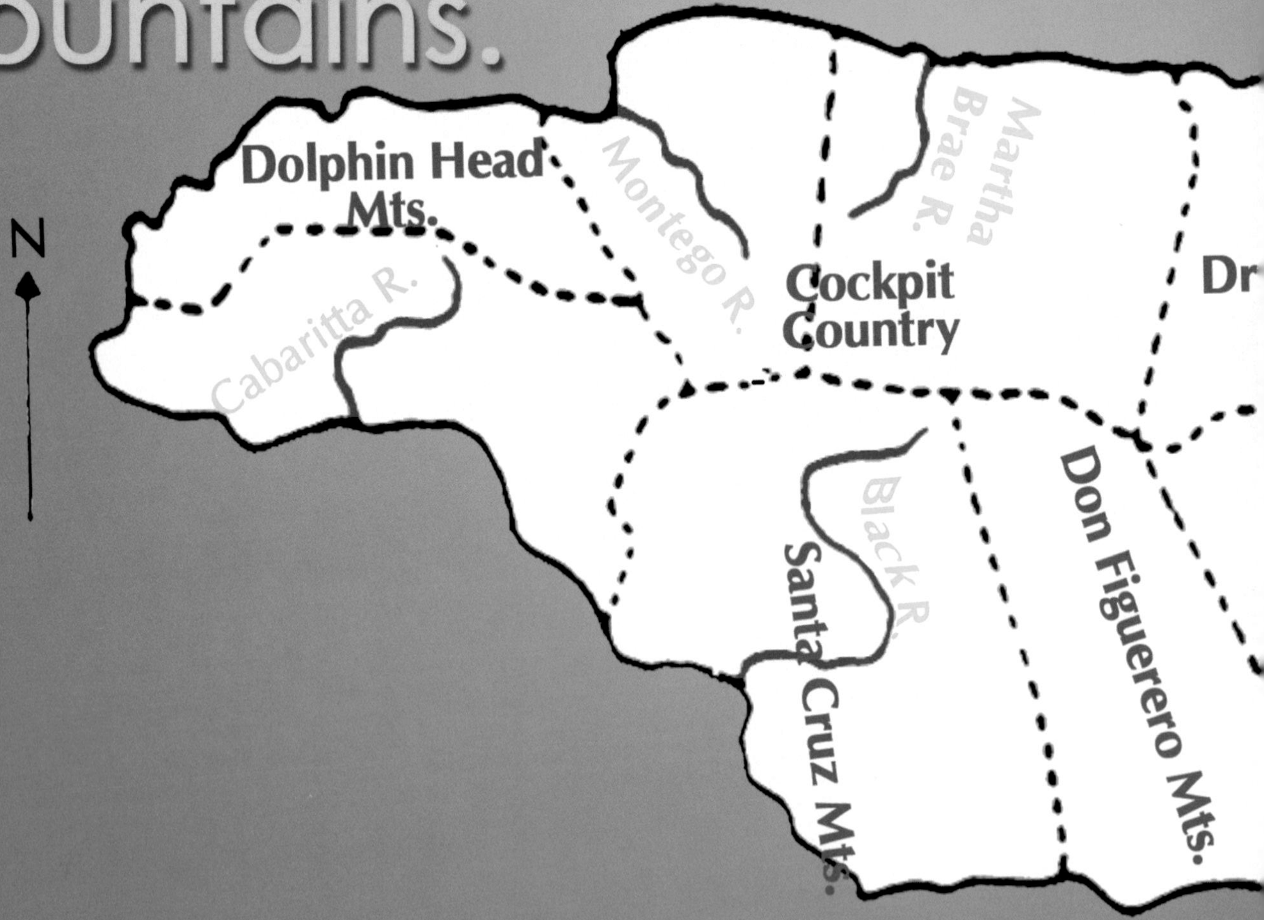

Dolphin Head Mts.

N

Cabaritta R.

Montego R.

Martha Brae R.

Cockpit Country

Dr

Santa Cruz Mts.

Black R.

Don Figuerero Mts.

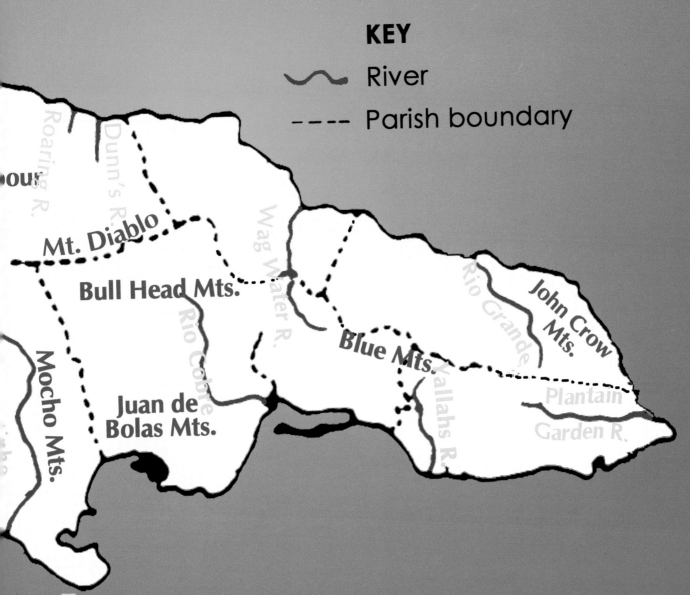

~ River

- - - - Parish boundary

Roaring R.

Dunn's R.

Mt. Diablo

Wag Water R.

Rio Grande

John Crow Mts.

Bull Head Mts.

Rio Cobre

Blue Mts.

Yallahs R.

Plantain Garden R.

Mocho Mts.

Juan de Bolas Mts.

Jamaica has many rivers.

Jamaica has three counties.
Each county has its own parishes.

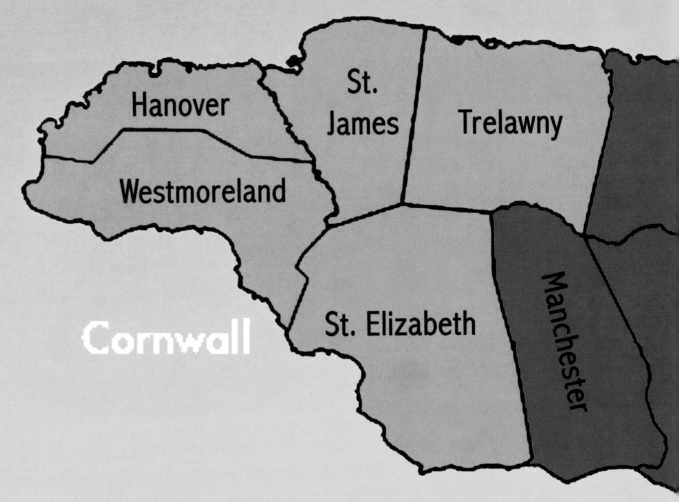

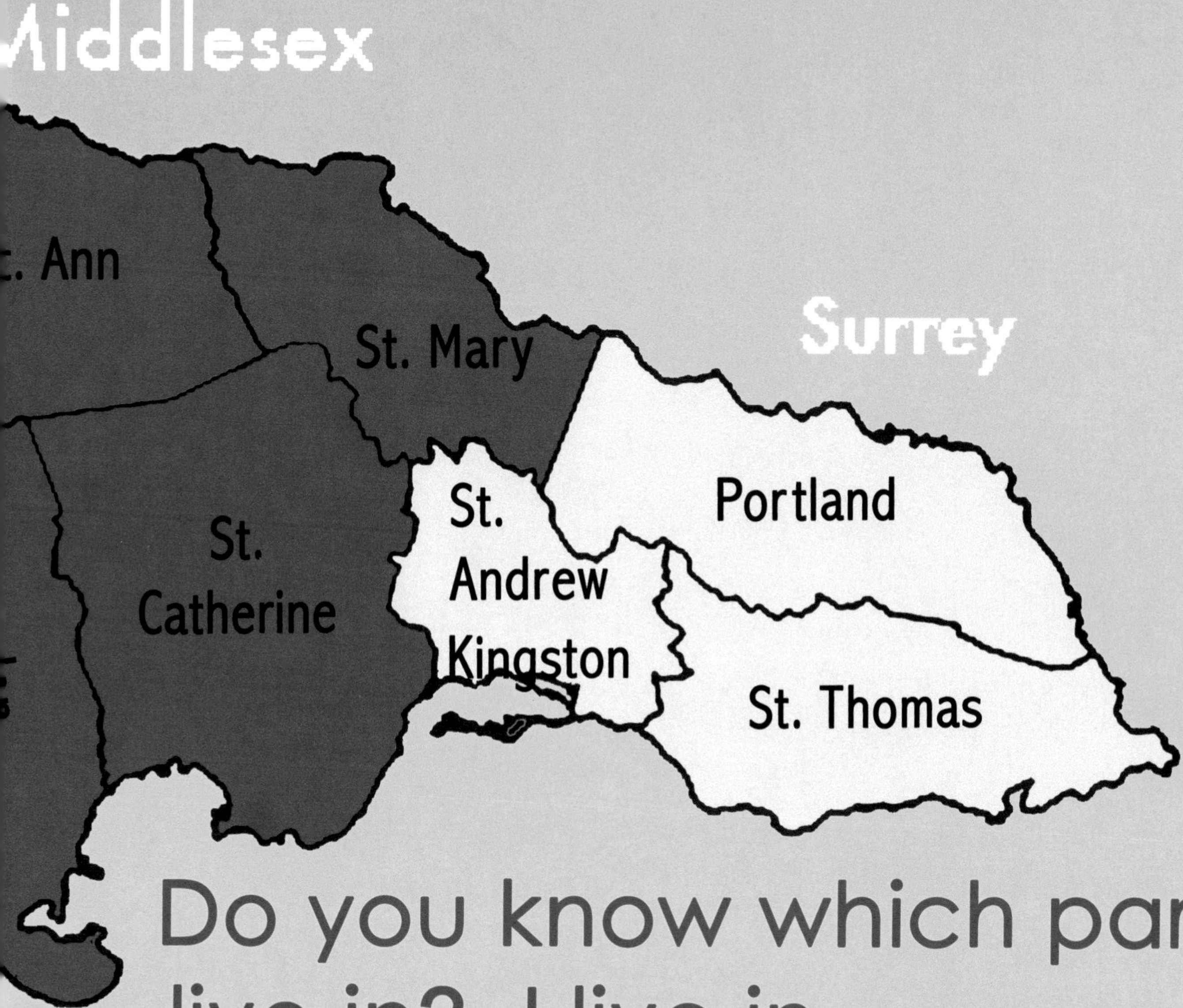

Middlesex

St. Ann

St. Mary

Surrey

St. Catherine

St. Andrew
Kingston

Portland

St. Thomas

Do you know which parish you live in? I live in _____.

The first people of Jamaica were the Tainos.

Then came the Spanish,

the English

and the Africans.

Next came
the East Indians

and the Chinese.

Over the years many people from the

Middle East have come to Jamaica to live and work.

These are the faces of some Jamaicans.

We all make up the motto,
"Out of Many, one People".

Jamaica has seven national heroes.

Right Excellent
Sam Sharpe

Right Excellent
Norman Manley

Right Excellent Sir
Alexander Bustamante

Right Excellent
Nanny of the Maroons

They all fought for our freedom.

Right Excellent
George William Gordon

Right Excellent
Marcus Garvey

Right Excellent
Paul Bogle

Jamaica has been an Independent country since August 6,1962.

The National Anthem

Eternal Father bless our land,
Guard us with Thy Mighty Hand,
Keep us free from evil powers,
Be our light through countless hours.
To our Leaders, Great Defender,
Grant true wisdom from above.
Justice, Truth be ours forever,
Jamaica, Land we love.
Jamaica, Jamaica, Jamaica land we love.

Teach us true respect for all,
Stir response to duty's call,
Strengthen us the weak to cherish,
Give us vision lest we perish.
Knowledge send us Heavenly Father,
Grant true wisdom from above.
Justice, Truth be ours forever,
Jamaica, land we love.
Jamaica, Jamaica, Jamaica land we love.

The National Pledge

Before God and all mankind, I pledge the love and loyalty of my heart, the wisdom and courage of my mind, the strength and vigour of my body in the service of my fellow citizens;

I promise to stand up for Justice, Brotherhood and Peace, to work diligently and creatively, to think generously and honestly, so that Jamaica may, under God, increase in beauty, fellowship and prosperity, and play her part in advancing the welfare of the whole human race.

The National Emblems of Jamaica

National Flag

National Bird
The Streamer Tailed
Humming Bird
(Trochilus Polytmus)

OUT OF MANY, ONE PEOPLE

Coat of Arms

National Flower
Lignum Vitae
(Guiacum officinale)

National Tree
Blue Mahoe
(Hibiscus elatus)

National Fruit
Ackee Fruit

38

Jamaica land we love.

About the Author

Dr. Adrian Mandara, experienced educator, author, motivational speaker and business administration consultant, has worked internationally for over forty years in his areas of specialization.

He holds a Ph.D. in Business Administration, emphasis in Marketing and Human Resource Development from Century University, Masters of Arts in Science and Comparative Education, Master of Science in Teaching and Curriculum and the Bachelor of Science in Education. His Graduate teaching was done at Bowling Green State University in the U.S.A. and at the University of Newcastle in England.

INTRODUCING THE
LMH QUICK READERS

The first in the series,

Festival Time, introduces

the reader to the

colourful, exciting,

fun-loving and

engaging spectacle

called Festival.

ALSO COMING IN THE
LMH QUICK READERS

42